am

i

too

broken?

Aryana Altaha

© 2023 Independently Published by
Aryana Altaha

All rights reserved.

ISBN 979-8850415006

Disclaimer: The following poetry book is based on the author's personal experiences with mental health and is not intended to provide medical advice. The author is not a mental health professional. While the book offers insights based on the author's individual journey, it is imperative to seek professional assistance for mental health concerns, as this book is not a substitute for medical or professional guidance. The author assumes no responsibility for any decisions or actions taken based on the content of this book, as it comprises solely of personal reflections.

to anyone who's ever felt too broken to be loved…

Table of Contents

1. Caged 7
2. Finally Flying 93

CAGED

empty promises

i learned to trust people's actions more than
their words
because how can you say you love me
when the only memories i have of you are all
connected to agony?

at first, i told myself all the menacing statements
you used to say to me
were one-time mistakes
because you **promised** you love me,
so why would you lie?

but as 1 time turned into 2 which turned into 10
i'd drive myself insane over and over again,
attempting to convince myself your promises
weren't empty
that your I Love You's were indeed true

but that became too hard to believe
when i started hating myself
trying to love you.

why?

sometimes the people i'm supposed to be the closest to
make me feel the most isolated

guilty pleasure

the only consistent source of comfort in my life
is the food i feel
too guilty
too fat
to eat
because the more it heals my soul
the more it eats away at my "health"
and the quicker it kills my body.

-eating my feelings away

the hate you give

you entered this world crying while everyone else was smiling.
you got so used to pain that you crawled like a parasite, spreading your metastatic disease.
you were fueled by envy, not admiration.
you'd always pity yourself instead of trying to fix yourself.

screaming with exhilaration, you wouldn't stop repainting the picture of failure on your friends' faces anytime they lost what was valuable to them.
and just like the devil, your secret source of relief was
"if i suffer, you suffer with me."

you'd find a way to never blame yourself for your hardships, thinking your hatred for everyone else would make your reality disappear.
all you'd ever do was silently cry yourself to sleep then complain that no one loves you.
you were right.
why would they?
your life is like a flower that blooms poisons of pain.
the hate you give.

am i too broken?

what you masked behind that beauty will forever rot my eyes.
and your lies blurred my already screwed-up perception.
worst of all, you'd idolize your suffering because that was the fastest route to what you valued most in this world—attention.

i stared at myself in the mirror one last time:
"the hate you give is why you were never happy."

and because of you
now i left this world smiling while everyone else is crying

-it wasn't because of the hate she gave but of the love she was never given

quiet burns

my days now blur
into a seamless wave of depression and
emptiness
followed by desperate attempts to achieve
goals
i don't work hard enough to finish.

life threw hell
but i couldn't adapt to the burning flames.
instead, i stood there and screamed
until my motivation ceased to exist
and my desires turned into ash.

they say water cools down burning flames
but the only water i've ever known
was the type that escapes eyes
that refused to open each morning
at the thought of this dreaded
infinite loop.

it's easy to give up
though that would cost me
my dignity and worth.

nowhere to go
nothing to give
everything to hide.

but the worst part is,
no one will ever know.
because after the countless
"don't worry. it's going to be fine"
i learned it's just better for the pain
to silently metastasize inside.

"why can't you just be happy?"

sometimes happiness is terrifying
because instead of savoring it as long as i can,
the only thought that crowds my mind is
"when will this high come to its inevitable end?"

2 minutes, 2 hours 2 days?
it's exhausting traveling through an
unpredictable roller coaster.

-when can i get off?

reflection

i'm sorry
how my eyes
remind you of the fear
he could inflict with just a slight stare

and how my lips
remind you of his words
that hit harder than his hands

i try not to care
because when you said i look like him,
that was something you just said
without a second thought

yet sometimes i can't help
but feel like a reflection of him
even though i should know i'm not.

-i am truly sorry.

numb

when you lose so many people,
there comes a point where you instinctively
emotionally detach yourself.

what used to feel like the deepest imaginable
wound
devouring my whole heart,
has turned into
a mere papercut.

i've learned to accept loneliness
because the sole "constant" in my life will only
ever be me.

leave me alone

have you ever been so scared of something
that it's the only thing you think of?
it never leaves your mind but rather stays
hidden,
then reveals itself at the slightest trigger.

sincerely,
your intrusive thoughts

no one warned me.

i used to idealize anxiety

i was told it's something everybody has,
a natural human characteristic.

no one warned me
about the nights i would spend
profusely sweating
yet still hiding under the covers
because i thought someone that didn't exist
would hurt me

no one warned me
that the pit of dread in my stomach would metastasize,
paralyze me with fear, and make me
cry
cry
and cry
until even the tears dried

no one warned me
about the nightmares that would replay
over and over again
of me being murdered in every possible way
all the escape routes i couldn't stop planning in my head

-anxiety isn't fun

cycles

it kind of hurts when you have to give up on
someone
that meant so much to you
because you know you mean nothing to them.

but can i really say
"lesson learned"
if it has turned
into an endless cycle?

a galaxy on fire

she tried to help
but that ended up being the one thing
she needed.

whenever she tried to fix someone else's world,
she'd watch her own crumble.

then at a distant view,
her eyes became paralyzed at what she saw
everything,
every memory,
every building,
brick by brick,
collapsed.

and there was nothing she could do:
abandon the world of someone she loves…
or her own?

both end in a tragedy.
if only she had help.

suddenly, her world turned nonexistent.

grief

it's agonizing how people can go on with their lives
meanwhile, every vein, every artery, every muscle is detaching itself from the rest of my body and ripping my heart from my chest.

school will still continue
the leaves will still fall
the bakery will still sell the same old overly dry muffins

as if nothing ever happened

i wish everyone suffered with me,
grieved with me.
i'd at least be comforted in my emotions
instead of being greeted with faces full of pity.

so i grimace in jealousy at someone else's joy
and can't help but smile at their agony.

"at least i'm not alone."

living vs surviving

i often wish i was never ambitious
so that i stop burdening myself with guilt

maybe, just maybe
if that was the case,
i'd understand what it means to thrive
instead of just simply survive

puppet

your magic was simply manipulation

but once i noticed it was already too late.
you already knew all my flaws

i'm now a puppet under your control.

you make me feel stupid

i love you
you broke me

all i wanted was to see you happy
all you did was use me

you did teach me a lot which made me stronger
but i wouldn't say i'm grateful for you

you'll never care which hurts because
you acted like you did

i thought i saw sincerity in your eyes
guess that really does show how love can make people blind

-why am i so naive?

forget but never forgive

they say time heals
but i disagree
time forgets
it forgets how inferior they made me feel about myself.

it forgets about how i'd start the day with dread
and end the night in tears

time slowly forgets memories–good or bad

maybe that's why i hold grudges,
to remember.

the internal scars they left on me.
it's evidence to prove that they don't deserve
my forgiveness.

but even grudges turn inferior to time because
no matter what
i'll eventually have forgotten
the taste of depression, of anxiousness, of anger
they inflicted

-time: a double-edged sword

ugly benefits

receiving benefits—the most desirable thing to a human.
but something so beautiful is an illusion
because once it's gone, we leave.

we fall in love because we receive the benefits.
compliments, attention, reassurance
but when it stops, so does our love.

we're selfish monsters
who can't recognize the beauty of love
so we illude it with the hideousness of
greedy ambition.

i cried out for help, and you came.
you fixed my wounds,
calmed my mind,
healed my heart,
and made me a stranger to the once
inseparable anxiety.

so, i loved you.
you were the miracle i needed and the savior of my life.

however, as time progressed,
the more my memory regressed.
the memories of the agony almost disappeared
so i didn't need you anymore.

that's why i left you,
not because you did anything wrong
but because i'm the villain.

-ugly benefits

what's the point?

"nothing good lasts forever"

so why waste your emotions
getting excited,
building love,
a deep connection,
over something you know will eventually
disappear?

"aren't you excited?"

i lost the ability to get excited because
*"if you expect disappointment,
you'll never be disappointed."*

-MJ

what my anxiety tells me

Number one:
make sure the doors are locked.
check
check again
check just one more time
it's locked; stop checking

Number two:
stay quiet
ignore them
they'll never understand you.
that'll only make you feel worse

Number three:
if you're not about to pass out,
you're not working hard enough.
don't romanticize burning out,
you need a break.

Number four:
what if i get hurt?
what if i'm never loved?
what if i never become successful?
what if…
you are what keeps me up at night.
let me sleep.

Number five:
what to do if someone points a gun at my head?
how do i perform CPR?
how do i survive a school shooting?
you've imagined enough fake scenarios.
please,
get some help

confused

i often ask myself whether
i'm a happy person who is sometimes sad
or a sad person who is sometimes happy

-i can't even understand my own emotions

why i hate you

i hate you
i hate you
i hate you

i hate even thinking about you
no words could fathom the years
of accumulated disgust that perpetuates
throughout my veins at the thought of you

but what made me hate you more
was knowing people would stare
as you rubbed salt into my wounds
and stabbed my soul a hundred times
then proceed to do nothing

watching me fight a goliath
but stand to the side and hope
i have the strength to deal with it myself

enablers, worst of them all.

addicted

it's crazy how quickly you can come to cherish someone
and the next second they become what you despise the most
manipulation

you thought it was love but your heart was filled with delusional admiration

took you long enough to realize.
but i shouldn't blame you
it's natural to yearn attention
the issue arose when it became addictive.

it's enjoyable in the moment
then turns into why you often switch to preferring loneliness

overshare, waste time, convince yourself of the timeless lie:
"they're different"

yearning your attention is like ecstasy
you gave me a high once i could never achieve again
it starts euphoric and ends with wretched withdraws

terrible timing

i finally feel like i deserve happiness

but i rejected it too many times before
so i guess it finally left.

-am i cursed?

please, listen

you hear me when i say i'm sick
but i need you to listen to me
believe me, accept it, and tell me
you will help me through it.

fight or flight

what i wish i say when someone asks:
"are you okay?"

No.
i stress myself out too much to the point where
my body doesn't know how to fight itself
anymore.
it desperately tries to fight against the ugly
truths i tell myself
you deserve it
it's all your fault
they don't like you
and i don't like you too

yet also tries to cover my ears in hopes
i don't hear these loud voices,
nurse me back to self love,
and feed me meaningless lies:
hey, i like you
stop beating yourself up
little you would be so proud of where you are
now

but i don't hear these stupid
attempting-to-comfort-me words anymore
even though i secretly crave it
i think it gave up and switched to flight mode
because it finally realized it was fighting a losing
battle

i don't blame you though.
you chose to flee
because i chose to ignore your desperate pleas.

so when someone asks if i'm okay
i'm sorry i lie when i say
"i'm fine"
it's just easier that way

i'm fine=i'm not fine

overprepared

i refuse to get hurt again
so i detach
it's my coping mechanism

i'm better prepared that way
because i already hurt myself
before anyone can

nuisance

i've sacrificed my own happiness and comfort
so that i don't make others feel uncomfortable
because if i do, they'll leave
they all leave

i've wasted my life pleasing people who treated
me like a temporary object

i am not temporary

so i like to think i'm better off alone
although i don't even make myself a priority

worth the risk

i fell in love with the idea of love
but whenever it shows up in real life
i can't help but hide

giving someone your all
hoping, praying, begging
they reciprocate it back
if they do, congrats
you found someone who's willing to share your pain
call everything you hate about yourself
nothing less than perfection,
bandage your internal wounds,
give you all the attention,
the type you'd read about in books and
desperately yearned to have someday

but if they don't reciprocate their love back
you have to act like it's okay
as if your whole world, your whole heart isn't under attack
because you'll still be able to survive anyway right?

-is it really worth the risk?

losing your light

i gave him my telescope
to show that
i'm starting to appreciate
my galaxy

but he began
magnifying my scars
and shutting down
my stars

in hopes of
making his
brighter

-i was starting to appreciate myself, so why did you try to disintegrate it?

mental corpse

you didn't die
but i still grieve
over who you were
or rather the person my mind
made you out to be

so i try
to bury you
into the rest of the memories
i wish to forget

-back to the beginning, loneliness

constant comparison

when i look at her
i feel like a shadow
whose only use is to
make her even brighter than she already was

how can i believe other people

when they tell me
"you're so special"
"unique"
"one of a kind"

when i look at me
hatred hijacks my mind
chills chase my body
and self disgust wishes
this shadow and i
would disappear and
blend into the darkness

the therapist friend

i love the rain
it offers to feel your sadness
and wash away the pain.

so i try to be that for others
and dry away their tears.

but when will my rain come
to wash away my fears?

how much is enough?

will you ever be proud of me?

if i achieve my goals, *i am lucky*
if i don't, *i am lazy.*

how much do i have to do for it to ever be enough to you?

-your insecurity

never enough

dear insecurity,

stop trying to justify laziness through self-pity,
it's nothing less than revolting.

-your academic validation

toxic perfectionism

i'm content so what's the point in working hard anymore, right?
should i convince myself i'll never amount to anything?
force myself to work harder until
the tired voices in my head scream at the top of their lungs for me to finally rest?

only then i'll be good enough
desperate enough
to win

you can never
rest
be proud
feel assured

there is *always* someone who will take your spot
the moment you stop fighting for it
so whether you cry blood or hear a million voices

you will not stop working until everyone else competes for second place
because you will always get first

it's toxic, but it works.

permanently broken

"how long will my depression stay?"

maybe i've always been this way
but desperately distracted myself
to make the emptiness go away

show & tell

isn't it strange?
how easily the way you treat me
can change

you say you love me
but the next second
you make me question
if you actually know what love is.

so here is my suggestion

don't tell me you love me,
show me you love me

experiencing your extremes

just the thought of you could make me smile
now it makes me grimace in regret

i could have never imagined my life
without you in it
now i'm grateful you left

deja vu

it's all deja vu
we argue about the same things
yet expect the outcomes to be something new

god, i thought i was less childish than this

-*talk* to me, don't *yell* to me

break the cycle

"abused become abusers; either you can learn from their mistakes or repeat it."

but isn't that so much pressure to place on a little kid?

it's not difficult to normalize the feeling
of nonstop pain and being betrayed
because when you witness destructive behavior so often,
it's almost imprinted in your DNA.

but i want to be good.
i want to be the someone
people think of when they imagine
their safe place.
not the someone who weaponizes innocence,
shoots happy hearts,
and kills their inner child.

god, don't let me become who i fear most
you can't let me turn out that way.

so take all my pent up wrath and burn it
because i can't allow someone else to pay
for something they never did

-they don't deserve it and neither did i.

are we the same?

when i get angry
it hijacks my body
and devours my control.

i feel it all over
it swallows me whole
so anything i say or do
isn't me anymore

even i can't deny
i look just like my dad, don't i?

care for yourself too

i disregard the words i preach
"know your worth"
but i'm still trying to find mine.

i gave it my all
what more do you want me to give?
am i just wasting my time?

you tell others how beautiful they are
throughout their highs and lows,
but you can't even do the same for yourself
the mirror reflection sighed,
"you're the biggest hypocrite i know"

escaping disappointment

"you have so much potential"
and now i have so much pressure

because if you don't live up to
everyone's expectations of you
you. are. pitied.

and nothing is more
pathetic than pity

a crowd of faces that scream
"i'm sorry"

yet secretly whisper
*"you should feel sorry for yourself,
there's so much you could've done
but never did."*

-*"i'm disappointed"*

overcontrolling

i wish i never let you control my mood,
my mind
i wish i didn't care all the time

"family" isn't a free pass

they say *"blood is thicker than water"*
but just because we share the same blood
doesn't mean it's okay
to say everything that's wrong with me
leech off my vulnerability
and suck my self worth away.

just because we share the same blood
doesn't mean your words never hurt
like a parasite that's slowly killing me inside
and withers my cells
like it withered the little love i had for myself.

why can't you see?
that just because we share the same blood
doesn't mean you don't have to apologize
for everything you've done to me.
you treated me like an object
that's been misused.

just because we share the same blood
doesn't mean your actions are excused.

my inner child

i hate how i pretend to act normal

all i want is to regress into a child
collapse into someone's arms
and be repeatedly reassured that
everything is going to be okay

but there is no one to convince me of such a
beautiful lie
so instead i try to pray
to a god i half believe in
"please save me"
"will everything truly be okay someday?"

on-off

it's a switch i can't control
one day i'm hollow
no remorse
no guilt
no empathy
i *cant* care

the next i feel full
with pure pain, sadness, solitude.

i go days on end without feeling anything
and then on a random night
i crash.

and suddenly
all the emotions come catching up to me
but the thing is
i didn't even know i was running away in the first place
it just...*happened.*

disguised truths

i used to joke that the easiest way
to deal with problems
is to run away from them
but i don't think i was joking

-the only way past it is through it

i'm so tired

what if i dont want to
allow myself
through and past the pain?

-let me escape

manipulation

i can't remember anything i did wrong
yet i can't help but feel such a strong sense
of nauseating conviction
as if all the agony he caused is my fault

manipulation.

limited vocabulary

"you hurt me"
3 words you can't understand
or maybe you just want to conceal
so instead you say i victimize myself
when all i did was acknowledge
how you made me feel

-"i'm sorry" 2 words i hope you learn how to use

toxic relationship

"you deserve better"
i know.
but that means i will have to let go
of all the highs
if i don't want to experience the lows

i don't think love should be
a constant emotional roller coaster
but i don't want to get off

-addicted

should i believe you?

i don't hate you
i just have nothing to say
to you anymore

should i try to forget those
memories of you from before
and remember you as someone new?
are you sure you won't
go back to the old you?

how do i know if you've truly changed
or if you're simply acting like you did
to erase the guilt?

-letting you in or letting you go

muse

you used to be the person
i endlessly admired
now you're the exact opposite
of who i want to be

overly-insecure

someone told me to be quiet today
and i don't know why but in my mind
that moment has been stuck on replay
so i tell myself i shouldn't have said that
i was too loud
too annoying
too comfortable
too much like myself
but why do i care so much?

-i need help. i don't know how to love myself

let me find you

i want to find the me that loves me
but how much longer do i have to search?

-please stop hiding from me

i can't breathe

breathe in.
breathe out.
if you want to be less anxious,
you need to allow yourself to
breathe.
just.
breathe.

but i can't stop suffocating myself.

i'm scared if i breathe,
i'll breathe too much.
i'll stop worrying
then stop working
not do anything
and everything i've done up until then
would all be for
nothing.

-i'm too scared to breathe.

mental < physical pain

if your body gets a cold
and you don't know what to do
you ask for help
now you're healthy
like you used to be

but if your soul goes cold
and your mind catches a fever
that matches your burning heart
from all the depression, anxiety, voices,
intrusive thoughts

and you don't know what to do,
if you ask for help
now you're weak

*"you don't even know how to help yourself,
god, i feel bad for you."*

why is it acceptable if my body hurts and not my heart?

-mental illness shouldn't be taboo

sick, not stupid

if i could simply smile my depression away or
if i could breathe my anxiety away
if it truly was that simple
do you really think it would still be called an illness?

it's mental *illness*
it is a *sickness*
not a phase i made up for attention

-i'm ill, not idiotic

too many mistakes

i hate that you care so much
and how you let your little heart
get hurt because of that

so you try to make it up to yourself
by leaving everyone else
the moment you see them
not care as much

avoid, ignore, detach
all of the above
but all that does
is turn you into an
emotionless
flat face
dull shadow
who only knows
how to push people away
then wonder why they don't love you

-i can't seem to do anything right, can i?

useful existence

do you care about me?
or am i merely something
you can benefit from?

-tell the truth even if it stings

self doubts

"try your best"
but what if it is not enough?
and what if it never will be?

that's why giving up
sometimes sounds more promising

at least that way
i will waste less time
trying something that
i know i'll never achieve anyway

why i fear death

people are taught to ignore death for as long as possible because
"why fear the inevitable?"

i can't help it though.
it disgusts me.

i could spend years calculating how i'm going to make enough money to survive,
i could spend years studying to get into the "best" schools,
i could spend years practicing over and over and over to win every single competition,
sacrificing my social life to be the best and become the person people admire the most.

but within a second,
every memory i had
or someone had of me
tear
smile
paranoid thought
worry
relationship
ounce of pain
will be ashes or a corpse that's slowly being eaten away.
how could you not grimace at such a thing?

"describe yourself."

a canvas that's covered in grey
but every type of shade
to match the empty thoughts
the lifeless tears
the feeling of constantly being devoured by
stress

-how do i define myself without the sadness?

hypocrite

i get mad at others when
they can't understand me
yet i can't even understand myself

uncontrollable, unpredictable

"do you even love me?"
i don't know

some days
i feel like my life
would be fine even
if everyone disappeared
yet some days that's
my greatest fear.

sometimes i do love you
and there's nothing
i want more than your presence.
other times i couldn't care less
about your absence.
sometimes that's what i crave.

it's like a switch that
constantly
turns on and off
and i don't know
how to make it stop

-emotional detachment vs attachment

the perfect child

the one every kid envies
who gets into an ivy league *(preferably Harvard)*
and becomes a doctor

the one who follows their parents' dreams even
if that means sacrificing their own.
winning competitions is expected
straight A's is the only acceptable answer
and a B? deplorable.

and when these "necessities" aren't met,
the only explanation is laziness.
and the moment you show "weakness"
there will be another kid who will replace your spotlight.

-mom, your baby is exhausted.

burnout

i can't even ask myself
"haven't i given enough?"
i know i haven't.
but i'm too exhausted to give any more

everything would've worked out if i did

but i still try to act like i've given it my all
to shield myself from the guilt
that reminds me
how disappointed it is

"you could've been everything you wanted to be"
"you could've been so much, yet you chose to be lazy"

double-edged words

poetry used to be my outlet
it mended the words i felt too broken to say,
and illustrated the beauty in expression.

but even a source of comfort
has turned into a building block
that's part of my city of anxiety
that's why sometimes i wish i was in pain
or else i'd conjure it myself

because with every ounce of agony,
is an opportunity to become a poetic
masterpiece.

i hate that i miss you

sometimes i wish i never left
now i have so much space to breathe
now my mind is almost empty
because you controlled most of my thoughts

there's no one constantly by my side anymore
to keep me up at night.
so lonely,
but at least now i can finally sleep

whenever i miss you i try to remember
how you made me feel.
like a prisoner who begged to be set free
but never tried to escape
because they never knew they could

you are what i hate
and i thank myself every day
for being the one who decided to leave

-dear anxiety…

guarded

giving my heart to somebody again
is like falling with no safety net
so i leave first before they can
because the risk of death is too high
the only difference is that
in one only your body is killed
in the other it's your heart, your soul, and your mind.

refuse to fall

im terrified to give it my all.
all my
flaws
fears
needs
tears
past
pain
imperfections
is that okay?
are you willing to work through it all?
i want to fall in love with someone
and experience how beautiful it can be
but i don't know what healthy and happy love
looks like
and i'm scared no one will catch me.

when daydreams turn into nightmares

you could make me the happiest...
or saddest girl in the world
depending on your mood
you're now the reason i believe in karma

i like to think i'm a kind person
but at the same time i pray
you get hurt the same way you hurt me
so that you learn to stop breaking hearts
and going on self-esteem killing sprees

i wish i could tell my younger self to prepare
for the pain that would ensue
and i hope one day you finally become aware
that you were the one who turned
my daydreams into nightmares

finally free

i hope you feel
what i felt
when you made me believe
that i was nothing
well now,
you're nothing to me.

"what does depression feel like?"

it's like a mind that is empty
but a heart that is full
of pure sadness, regret, anger, despair
that combine into a numb, debilitating pain
which seeps into gaps of the brokenness it
caused.

oversimplifying

i know medication is important
but don't expect these
countless pills
to suddenly heal
all the pain i feel

-illness isn't always that simple

ent # **FINALLY FLYING**

first time flying

accepting help is like
learning how to fly for the first time.
you could thrive
soaring
absorbing all the majestic views
you couldn't see before.

or

fall,
fall further into a pit of loneliness
that's deeper than you ever imagined.
be misunderstood
not taken seriously
blamed for feeling this way

but
i think i'm finally flying
i'm not afraid to fall
i learned not to be
and even if i do…

someone, my safety net, once told me
"i'm here and always ready to catch you"

-finding people who care

moon cycles

i always admired the moon

it goes through
different phases of emptiness
but eventually
always ends up whole again

-when i grow up, i want to be like the moon

fact vs opinion

their opinion
of you is
not
a fact.

-it doesn't define you and it never has

it's okay to be excited

if you can imagine the worst
you can imagine the best.

-what if you don't get disappointed this time?

i can finally breathe

we could sit in silence
yet you still make me
feel heard.

even when i can't feel anything
you feel it for me.

*"if you want to heal
you need to allow yourself
to feel"*

that's what you taught me

so thank you
for treating a hurting heart
with care.

after a long time
of suffocating myself,
i'm starting to breathe.
thank you for being
my breath of fresh air.

their gain isn't your loss

someone else's beauty
will never
take away from yours

"be humble"

self hatred
isn't
being humble

-loving yourself isn't something to be ashamed of

leaving abandoned love

just because you wait,
doesn't mean they're coming back.

self love
is
self discipline

i need you to realize that.
you can let yourself feel
but you need to let yourself let go

-it's hard but you deserve more than
someone who makes you feel unloved

loving the little things

you were the one who reminded me why i love
sunrises

it doesn't matter
whether i laugh so much
to the point where even the
rain is jealous of how much i cry

or a drought that dried
out every drop of hope
and left me stranded in
a pit of helplessness

or a sunny day
where the sky is blue.
so ordinary, too mundane to even care

but you taught me to notice
and love the little things

so i do.
now every time i look at the sky,
i'm reminded of you
because you will *always* be there.
you give me something to look forward to.

you are my sunrise.

-and i'm so grateful for you

sunrises

it could be the worst or best day of my life
it doesn't matter
because there will *always* be those
breathtakingly beautiful colors that paint the sky.
it's my hope, my peace.

the sun will *always* rise again
and so will you.

healing hearts

you convinced me to
love to live

and because of you,
i also live to love

now all i want
is for my love to one day
help heal someone's wounds
and teach them to love their scars
like how you taught me to love mine

-you helped fix a broken heart that you didn't even break

do i deserve this?

how am i supposed to react to someone's constant support?

you make me feel so loved
and almost make me believe
i deserve to let go and let myself live.

but it feels so wrong for everything to be going so right.

i'm anchored by voices that tell me it'll all come crashing down
and they create this paralyzing fear
that forces me to push everyone away.
so why are you still here?

why are you willing to listen to me
translate these thoughts
and waste your time to hear every
overthinking, intrusive, dramatic
feeling i feel?

how are you so willing to tell me it's going to be okay
in 100 different ways?

i don't even think you understand how i feel,
yet you still try to.

why do you care about me so much?
and why am i so tempted to listen
when you tell me to let go?
let go of every thought that screams in my ears
i have to punish myself.

i want to let go and start again,
i really do.

so thank you.
for being there for me
when i can't even be there for myself.

-mom, i found the person who i thought would never exist. i found my safe space.

hope

what if
it turns out
better than you
could have ever imagined?

-falling in love with hope

you do deserve it

"a picture is worth a 1000 words"

and your happiness is worth
every word. ever written.

-you deserve happiness

making myself happy

if you are here for me
i will smile

but if you are not
i will smile anyway
because i have me
and

i
will
never
leave me

-self love

seas of tears

if you are drowning
in your own thoughts
and wonder if you will
ever be saved,

reach out your hand.
and i will take it,
help you stay afloat,
and help drain your ocean
of overthinking away.

it's okay to not know how to handle
everything on your own.

necessary reminder

in case you haven't heard this in a while
i love you
all of you is pure beauty
from the way your heart gets so happy about
the little things
to the way you smile

you are so worthy of everything you want to
achieve
i'm so proud of you
and i hope one day you realize that
and you're proud of yourself too.

exquisite existence

once you realize
the true beauty of *your* existence
it won't matter if people say otherwise

-understanding your worth

loving the "boring love"

i was so used to fireworks
people who could turn my dark sky
into endless constellations
and make me so ecstatic
my adrenaline could explode

but i forgot fireworks quickly burn out
and the next second then
it would be dark again

but i think i finally found my warm fire
someone who warms my cold thoughts
and protects my healing heart.

-my happy place

i'm sorry.

i'm sorry for teaching you you'll only ever be
good enough
if you were the best
and whispering in your ears how disgusted and
disappointed i am
the moment you finally allowed yourself to rest

i'm sorry for making you feel guilty over
eating carbs
and making you cry because of
how hungry you are

i'm sorry for forcing you to hold in all your pain
till it inevitably spilled
but no one can notice
so you pushed away anyone who came

i'm sorry for convincing you no one will
understand
and making you feel alone
locking you away in your room
i wanted that place to feel like your safe space,
your home
but to you it meant isolation
hell
guess that really does show
i never took the time to know you that well

for a long time i continued to stare at the photo
of my younger self.

if only you knew what you'll go through.
i'm sorry for never being proud of you.
but i love you and i want you to know,
im starting to love myself too.

-i forgive you.

not everyone will appreciate

not everyone will appreciate
how much effort you put in
to make them feel loved

how you overshare to fill the awkward silence
and hopefully find a similarity to bond over

how you try to make them smile
hopefully laugh
even if that means embarrassing yourself

how you refuse to open up
because you don't want to burden them
and force their comfort onto you
to bandage your pain

or how you offer all your love
knowing they may never
reciprocate it back

not everyone will appreciate
how much you try
but that is not a reflection
of how worthy you are

because you are priceless
and i need you to understand that

questions i ask myself

what if
you achieve
all your goals
and everyone is proud of you?

will you finally be proud of you too?

constant voices

a million voices in my head
but your smile could silence them all

"smile so the universe smiles back at you"
-a Persian proverb

my vulnerability isn't weak

when i told you i'm seeking professional help
why did you laugh in my face?

everything that is wrong with my mind
isn't just something i can easily replace.

are you ashamed to be associated with me,
someone who finally collected the courage to be set free
from her own mind

my heart was already as fragile as glass
so you didn't have to break something
that i started trying to fix

but i will not apologize for not knowing
how to *"deal with it"* myself

because i deserve to express my vulnerability
without being scared of you
viewing me as weak.

telling eyes

when i ask you if you're fine
your mouth says no
but your eyes scream that that's a lie.

i know you secretly pray that someone would notice
well, i did.
and i know it's been rough
and i don't know how comforting this may be
but i need you to know that you will always and forever be enough

"it will get better day by day"

it will get better
but some days may be a lot worse than others.

because progress isn't linear

but after a while
happiness will start feeling
less like a stranger
and more like a close friend

you'll see it in the way you smile
you'll feel it when you realize life is more worthwhile
than you could have ever imagined.

and you'll know it because when those
"bad days" come
you'll lift yourself up
and keep on trying
and keep on living

-just keep swimming

you are allowed to feel

there will always be
someone who has it
"worse than you"

but that will never mean
what you're going through
is any less important

trauma doesn't always look like a sharp knife
100 needles can make you bleed to death too

*-your feelings have been, are, and will always
be valid*

childhood trauma

Parents,
give your child attention
if you don't, they may find it in
~~men~~ boys who teach them
they're nothing more than their bodies
drugs and drinks to distract themselves
from the disgusting taste of loneliness
good grades to make them feel worthy enough
and fill that void in their heart.

all we're asking for is
your love
your care
your protection

isn't that your obligation?

-am i really that hard to love?

fading scars

i'm finally getting help
aren't you proud?
i'm fixing the scars you gave me

the bare minimum.

don't beg to be given a star
when there is someone out there
who will give you
constellations
one day

just wait,
they are only a couple light years away

-*"we accept the love we think we deserve"*
The Perks of Being a Wallflower

a closed chapter

you can forgive someone
without allowing them
to enter your life
again

therapy lessons

-every behavior
is a need
yearning to be met

-don't punish yourself
for not knowing what
you hadn't learned yet

-things i learned in therapy

proper places

*"you can't heal
in the same environment
that made you sick"*

pain & peace

protect your peace
even if it means
some people cease
to be in your life

-realizing who cares
vs
who only acts like they do

answered questions

if you have to question
whether or not they are
good for you,
there's your answer.

if they were,
they wouldn't make you question it.

-don't settle for less when you deserve so much more

a heart's insight

the highs are too high
the lows are too low
too hectic
too lethargic
too drained to guess
which one it'll be anymore

i need stability
i need the ability
to say *"i'm fine"*
and mean it.

imagine your heart rate
if you were fine all the time
only ever "in the middle"
just like you wished
you would flatline.

let yourself live; you deserve it

it will be okay
so *please* let go
of the thoughts that nonstop worry about
tomorrow
the day after
and the rest of the days that proceed

"what if something bad happens?"
"what if someone does something to me?"

"what if"–those 2 words will kill you someday
they'll rob you of the happy life you deserve
if you don't throw them away

-please let go and focus on what you can control

losing you

if you surround yourself with people
who don't see your value,
soon you'll lose sight of it too

please, whatever you do, don't give up

sometimes some things
have to get worse
before they get better

but
it will
get better

-"what's one thing you wish you could tell your younger self?"

agonizing advice

i hate to admit it
but sometimes the most painful experiences
are the ones i'm most grateful for.

it taught me:
what i love
what i hate
who i love
who i hate
what i want but don't need
who cares about me
who doesn't
how to exist
how to live instead of merely exist

it was only going through hell that i was forced
to find
what i wanted my true heaven to be.

-blessings in disguise

reflections of love

learn to love yourself
before loving someone else
instead of letting their love for you
reflect how much
you're allowed to love yourself

time to let go

if you need to
allow yourself to grieve your past
but you do need to
allow yourself to move on from it.

you can't let yourself stay stuck on something
you will never be able to change

-you deserve more respect than that

and they will come

if you could love
the wrong person
so much

just imagine how much you can love
the right one

people pleasing

it will always be okay to lose people
trying to find yourself.
it will never be okay to lose who you are
trying to please other people.

haunted

i fear regret more than rejection.

"rejection is redirection"
and i agree.

regret drills itself into your heart
and you try to block it out
but the only thing that makes are holes
for all your integrity to leak out
until what's left is a shriveled heart
that can't respect itself

-i refuse to have any more regrets

working overtime

it's not your job
to make them
love you

hearts brighter than stars

when someone loves you
they will try and help you love yourself
show you your scars are constellations
that map the way to your bright heart.

they will help you love your stars
not burn them out.

-if someone loves you, they shouldn't make you hate yourself

discipline

i've decided that my self respect
will come before my feelings

so even if i love you
if you make me feel unloved
i need to let you go

because i know
there is someone out there
who will love me
maybe even more than i deserve

there is a difference

prioritizing
yourself
is not
selfish.

Kintsugi:
the Japanese art of mending broken
pottery, highlighting the cracks in gold,
and recognizing the beauty in
reconstructing shattered fragments.

you will heal
you are not "too broken"
you will *always* be worthy of love

Printed in Great Britain
by Amazon